BRING ʸᵗ DISNEᵽ ᵗᵘ ᵽᵘᵘᴿ NEXᵽ EVENᵽ

M000073181

If you find value here and, hopefully, found me to be an interesting and   engaging guy, consider having me come speak at your next event. Visit www.VanceMorris.com.

"If you're looking for a speaker to bring value to your group, I would strongly suggest you talk to Vance Morris."
Bill Gough, BGI Systems

HAVE ᵽᵘᵘᴿ NEXᵽ EVENᵽ Aᵽ DISNEᵽ

Looking for an event for your group or association? My 3-Day "Service Accelerator Boot Camp" in Orlando at the Walt Disney World Resort gives you the blueprint to Disnify your business, through classroom instruction, in park experiences and access to current Disney Leadership. Visit www.VanceMorris.com/

If you're looking for an easy, high value, and fun event for your niche, this is a home run."

Kris Murray, Owner

Child Care Marketing Solutions

---

www.DeliverServiceNow.com

Tales From The Customer Service Crypt

Tales From The Customer Service Crypt

10 Tales of Customer Experiences So Poor, They Should Be Buried In a Crypt For All Eternity

AND

47 Strategies, Questions, or Tactics You Can Use Right Now to Improve Your Client / Patient Experience

Vance Morris

www.DeliverServiceNow.com

Also by Vance Morris:

Systematic Magic. 7 Magic Keys to Disnify Your Business

7 Rules For Business Prosperity In Any Economy

Dedicated to my daughter Emma. She bravely stood by me, without embarrassment or shame, while I got my picture taken with every Disney princess.

Table of contents

About This Book

Growing up, I loved watching Tales From The Crypt. The show was a series of horror stories told by the "Crypt Keeper". It was slightly terrifying, usually humorous and always had a lesson or moral to the story.

This book is much the same as the show.

- Cringe (terrifying) worthy
- Usually humorous
- Always a lesson or moral

Unlike "Tales from the Crypt", the stories contained here in this book are ALL REAL experiences.

- Not embellished
- Not over-blown
- Not fiction

Throughout this book, you will find a symbol like this ⇒ . It indicates the lesson or moral as well as questions you should be asking yourself about that chapter.

Take the time to truthfully answer any questions posed here. Jot down ideas. Create to-do lists.

But most important... Implement.

Regards,

Vance "The Crypt Keeper" Morris

"Vance was instrumental in the redesign, opening and operation of Chef Mickey's at the Contemporary Resort. Working with the Chefs, Entertainment and other WDW Resort stakeholders, Vance implemented the core Disney Service Standards throughout the restaurant and even improved some of those systems for greater efficiency.

His understanding of Disney's philosophies and mission helped create the premier character dining destination at Walt Disney World."

Charles Henning
Vice President, Walt Disney World

"I worked with Vance Morris to create an incredible Disney Service Boot Camp event for my clients and members in early childhood education.

We not only sold out the event from stage in just a few minutes, we oversold it to the point where we had to add another trip!

The seminar itself was a unique blend of "classroom" time mixed with onsite tours of both Magic Kingdom and Epcot.

Vance is great to work with and everything was "turn key" for me as the host, which was greatly appreciated.

If you're looking for an easy, high value, and fun event for your niche, this is a home run."

Kris Murray, Owner
Child Care Marketing Solutions

"In a world awash in poor or nonexistent customer service, it is rare to find someone who so thoroughly understands the importance of a superior customer service experience and how to engage your employees in creating a system that works like magic.

Vance Morris is our go-to resource for improving the service of our own private practices and the practices of our coaching clients throughout the world.

If you want some "rah-rah" inspiration and motivation on customer service, you can pick up any one of the thousand worthless books on Amazon, but if you want to see real, tangible results in your own business with customers, patients, clients or donors who stay, pay and refer to you like "magic" then call Vance Morris and get on his waiting list.

No one knows this area more than Vance."

Dr. Dustin Burleson

Founder, Burleson Orthodontics & Pediatric Dentistry

President and Senior Consultant, Dustin Burleson Seminars

15

"We hired Vance as a speaker at one of our events – – from the moment that we decided we were gonna hire him until the moment he left the stage, Vance did an incredible job of delivering value to both me as the host and also to our attendees.

Vance volunteered to write articles for us for our newsletter to include so we could warm the audience and our attendees up prior to Vance coming on stage. He did a great job with those two, by the way. We even interviewed him for a teleconference.

And, so, when Vance was there to speak, our people were kind of made aware of who he was and what he could do to wow them.

So, his talk on how to Disnify any business on improving your customer service was fantastic, so much so that he got a great standing ovation at the end of it.

So, if you're looking for a speaker or someone that you can interview to bring value to your group, **I would strongly suggest you talk to Vance Morris.**"

Bill Gough
BGI Systems

Vance Tries To
Send A Fax

We were so close, yet so far from a true Disney Experience. Earlier this year, I was at a convention for one of the other businesses I own, staying at a non-Disney hotel on Disney property.

I guess they were just trying to save a buck, but those savings were far overshadowed by the hotels failure to come even close to A Real Disney Experience.

Now maybe it is just me... I did after all, spend 10 years as a Service Manager at various REAL Disney properties. So I may be a bit hyper-critical... I am definitely **INTOLERANT** of poor service and follow-up, and I have always OVER-MANAGED.

Here are a couple of the interactions I had during my stay at convention (Guess which was REAL Disney and which was NOT)

Bus driver complaining out loud to a bus full of people *"I wish these slow*

Disney bus drivers would get out of my way". Moments earlier he was doing 50 mph in a 35 zone. The "slow" Disney buses were going 35 mph.

The lady selling Churro's gladly signing my daughters autograph book.

The restaurant hostess greeting us with "We're closed". No offer to direct us to an open location where I wanted to spend money and god-forbid tip someone.

My wife buying her favorite coffee drink (a complicated coffee), which rang up $9.00, and having the clerk – what do they call them? Barristas? Coffee artists? – say to her: "Wow, that's expensive."

And #5 is a doosy....

Vance tries to send a fax

Before the first session of my convention, I had gotten up early to get some work done. At about 5:30 am I went down to the front desk of this VERY UN-Disney hotel to send a one page fax. The Front Desk Person refused to send a fax for me "*Cause the business office is closed*".

Me: "*So you mean to tell me the only time I can send a fax in the hotel is between 8 and 4:30?* I asked incredulously.

So I tried a different tact:

Me: "*Can you at least tell me if you **have** a fax machine*".

Her: "*Yes, Sir, right here under my desk.*"

Me: "*Do you know how to **use** the fax machine?*" I prodded.

Her: "*Of course, sir*"

Me: "*Since the business office is closed, could I give you a dollar for your troubles and have you send this one page fax?*"

Her: "*Ohhh, I don't know. I don't have any way to ring in the dollar into our system.*"

At this point I am ready to slap myself a la Homer Simpson and scream DOH!

Me: "Is *there anyone in this entire hotel that has the power, juice and authority to operate the fax machine sitting between your legs?*

Her: "*Yes let me get my manager*"

In comes the manager...

Her #2: *How may I help you sir?*

Me: *I would like to send this one page fax with your fax machine.*

Her #2: "*Well, sir, guests are only allowed to use the fax in the business office*". "*Security Reasons*", **she #2** continued.

Is there a defibrillator in the house?

At this point I am <u>apoplectic</u>... As my blood begins to boil, I grit my teeth and strain my lips a little song starts playing in my mind ("Beauty & The Beast's Be our guest, Be our guest, Put our Service to the test)

Me: *How much does it cost you to send a fax?*

Her #2: "*I have no idea*"

Me: *"Can we agree that it would be about a buck?"*

Her #2: *"Well, of course... That seems like a lot of money to send a fax."*

Me: *"Well, if I give you a dollar, and you agree that I am OVER paying for this service, could you please send the fax? Your hotel is definitely making a profit on this transaction"*

Her #2: *"Well, I don't have a way to ring up this sale, so I don't think I can do it."*

WOW!!! A hotel company would risk losing the business of a client over the sending of a ONE PAGE FAX!

So guess what my next step was... Go find a REAL Disney employee. So I walked across the street to Downtown Disney, which is really a part of the company.

The first guy I saw there was Randall who was sweeping up leaves. (Remember it is about 5:30 am). I asked Randall if his supervisor was around. He said "Yes", but also asked if he could help me.

I told him that I needed to send a fax and that the hotel was refusing to do so.

Randall: *"Well, we have a fax machine in our Housekeeping office. I am sure we could send it from there"*

So we walked over to their office and Randall invited me in. Evidently I was not a security risk to him.

Randall: *If you would give me the number, I can send the fax for you".*

Me: *You don't need a supervisor?"*

Randall: *To send a fax? Nah... they let me do it. My boss would look at me funny if I asked him if I was allowed to send a fax for a guest. I mean it is not hard and it doesn't cost a thing"*

And so Randall sent my one page fax.

Happy Ending (for me)

I tried to give Randall a tip, but he graciously declined (as I knew he would). But I did send a letter to both Disney and The Palace Hotel describing my travails and praising Randall.

I have already received a return letter from the Housekeeping Manager at Downtown

Disney, thanking me for my comments about Randall.

It has been 35 days since I sent my letters...

Still no reply from the Palace Management....

Don't think I will ever get one...

Do you have ridiculously stupid rules, regulations or policies that get in the way of serving your clients?

NOW is a good time to start rooting them out and eliminating them.

⇒ Do you give your team the flexibility and latitude to make decisions on their own that will only enhance your level of service?

⇒ Or.... Do you have a couple of "Hers" working for you?

⇒ Go and find the "hers" working in your practice and do something about them.

How Was Your Flight?

Being a national speaker and consultant puts me on a lot of planes every year. Some air lines down right suck (American, US Air, and Spirit) with their horrible on-time rates (just try to get a US Air shuttle out of La Guardia to Washington DC and not be delayed HOURS) to their very perfunctory flight attendants and air crews.

Not one person focusing on the customer experience. Just get the plane in the air and back on the ground again, skip the courtesies, this is a business.

Compare that with Jet Blue or Southwest.

Both airlines, care about the customer experience in their own ways. Southwest is famous for the stand up comic routine of the flight attendants

"For those of you who have not been in a car since 1963, this is a seatbelt" during the pre-flight safety instructions.

Both airlines make you feel comfortable and try to give you a happy flight.

After a flight, the most common question I get from the company that is hosting me is "*How was your flight?*"

I assume that many if not all, the folks on that flight will be asked the same question. That's 175 people getting asked the same question about one airline.

That same kind of question is often asked of your clients after you deliver a service or product.

Their friends and neighbors will ask:

"*How was the dentist?*",

"*How was the carpet cleaner?*"

These questions can only be answered in one of three different ways:

1. They will say something nice about you and your business:

"Vance, how was your flight?" It was great, you'll never guess what the flight attendant said, they were on time and the pilot gave us a great tour of the East Coast." "WOW! What airline were you on?" And from there a conversation is started.

2. They will say nothing about you and your business.

"Vance, how was you flight? "It was OK".

No conversation ensues.

3. They will say something derogatory about you and your business.

"Vance, how was your flight?" "I can't begin to describe how rude and surly the flight attendant was..." And then the delays... And no apology for the delays... Then there was no ice..." "WOW! What airline were you on?" and from there a NEGATIVE conversation is started.

As Walt Disney always said, *"Our business must be tellable".*

That is true.

But in what context do you want your business "told about"?

What customer experience do you want them to have?

If you asked someone about your business, what conversation would be had or would there even be a conversation as in answer #2 above?

Breastraunts

Love em or hate em, breastraunts, those restaurants who cater mostly to men and employ scantily clothed young, female servers are generating incredible sales and profits, even as other casual restaurants are sagging and dying.

What's this got to do with your business?

Why is a Disney Guy talking about breastraunts?

Don't fret, I will tie it all together in a neat little bow soon enough.

Recently, thinkprogress.org ran an article about a case study breastraunt called Twin Peaks (yes, pun intended).

They were also at the center of the brewhaha involving the bike gangs in Texas, but I am not covering that.

This restaurant franchise was launched in 2005 as an alternative to the skimpily orange attired Hooters. Twin Peaks was the fastest growing chain restaurant in 2013.

What makes them so successful?

The bottom line is that they know and understand their target market; men. "Men are simple creatures"' stated the twin peaks spokesperson, "so you don't have to go crazy getting them in the door."

Beer, sports and beautiful women are all it takes.

But their market targeting goes much deeper, according to leaked internal memos. They not only know their demographic profile, but more importantly, the psychographic profile.

The restaurant targets men "who love to have their ego stroked by beautiful girls" and promises an environment that *"feeds the ego with the attention they crave"*.

They describe their typical customer as someone who like attention from beautiful girls and being recognized in front of the guys, as well as someone who doesn't want to be asked "what are you thinking?"

They also have a brand promise or mission statement that any employee can wrap their pea brains around. "daring to create an adventure guys can't live without".

They have correctly identified their raving fan as "*I am the man, I believe in freedom, bacon, working hard and playing harder. I deserve to drink a cold beer and catch the game without being asked what I'm thinking*".

So here is **<u>lesson number one</u>** and the reason you should be paying attention;

They know their target market intimately.

Down to the lowest emotional trait. They know what their target customer wants, who they are and they deliver.

Do you know your target market that intimately?

Have you invested the time searching, prodding and snooping about what makes your target market tick?

This relates directly to the Disney client compass; understanding and exploiting your clients needs, wants, emotions and sterotypes.

Disney studies and measures the wants and desires of its guests on an hourly sometime minute by minute basis. They then crunch that data and utilize it to further increase service, raise prices, change attractions, etc...

All to extract more money from each and every guest (without them feeling like they have been gouged or swindled).

<u>Lesson number two</u>.

They work in a niche, attracting their perfect customer and repelling people, mostly women, who do not fit in their brand vision "*a place guys can't live without*."

This is one reason they are growing so fast, enjoying their profits, while other casual style restaurants are dying off one by one, failing to differentiate themselves from one another.

Walk into a TGIFridays, Chilis, Ruby Tuesday, Applebee's, etc, and they all look the same. Same decor, same menu, same clientele, same sameness.

They are lost in a sea of sameness. Almost like they were all neutered, turned into a bland whiteout.

There is nothing else like Disney in the entire world.

They are in a category of one.

They stay true to their target market and mission statement by "*providing the finest in family entertainment*". Certainly not a Twin Peaks, but they know how to differentiate themselves.

What have you done to separate yourself from the competition?

Are you just like the rest the companies in your market or niche?

Have you created a differentiating factor that speaks directly to your target market, repelling all others, to create your raving fans?

In order for you to thrive in this economy, you must break from the pack of sameness. You must identify with your target market and be unrelenting in your pursuit of them and the repelling of anyone who is not.

Now...get me a beer... Pretty please?

Disney World Banning Childless Couples?!

Ohh... Baby... There is a giant kerfuffle on social media right now.

Evidently, back in September, some nutty lady went off the deep end and ranted about how childless people should be banned from Disney.

I am not sure why it just got picked up now, but the media has really pushed this story line for the past week or so.

The original post on Twitter, as of today has 73,000 likes and 18,000 shares.

NBC, FOX, CBS and all the major networks broadcast the story.

Opinion pieces have been written in major newspapers.

Bloggers have blogged.

Twitters have tweeted.

I have cleaned up some of it for my sensitive viewers.

September 22 at 1:04 AM

It pisses me off TO NO END!!!! when I see CHILDLESS COUPLES WITHOUT AT DISNEY WORLD!!!! 😡😡😡😡😡😡😡😡😡😡 DW is a FAMILY amusement park!!!! yet these IMMATURE millennials THROW AWAY THEIR MONEY ON USELESS CRAP!!!! They have NO idea the JOY and HAPPINESS it is to MOTHERS WHO BUYS THEIR BABIES TREATS AND TOYS!!!! THEY WILL NEVER EXPERIENCE THE EXHAUSTION THAT IT IS TO CHASE A 3 YEAR OLD AROUND AND GETTING STARES AT ASSUMING IM A BAD MOTHER!!!! ~~This slut in some very SLUTTY~~ shorts was buying a Mickey pretzel and Aiden wanted one but the line was very long so I said later and it broke his poor little heart and he cried I WANTED TO TAKE THAT ~~FUCKING PRETZEL FROM THAT TRAMP~~ LIKE THANKS ~~BITCH YOU MADE MY SON CRY~~!!! 😡😡😡😡😡😡 DW is for CHILDREN!!!! People without CHILDREN need to be BANNED!!!! Mothers with children should be allowed to skip ALL THE LINE!!!! YOU HAVE NO ~~FUCKING IDEA WHAT ITS LIK~~E TO HAVE TO STAND IN LINE FOR 3 HOURS WITH A CRANKY TIRED EXHAUSTED TODDLER!!!! AND I CANT JUST TELL HIM THAT WE CANT DO SOMETHING BECAUSE ITS HIS VACATION TOO!!!! I ~~fucking hate childless women~~ with a BURNING PASSION!!! 😡😡😡😡😡😡😡😡😡😡

People have bashed, defended and commented on this story over 1,000,000,000 times in the past week. No matter where you fall on the issue, this is a HUGE amount of FREE publicity for the company.

To get this kind of exposure, Disney would have to have spent hundreds of millions of dollars.

Look, the company has been courting adults for years, specifically millennials who have fond memories growing up in the amusement parks.

According to a recent report, at least three-quarters of millennials, 78% with children and 75% without, said they're planning on going to a theme park this year, compared with 58% of all adults, according to a 2018 survey from research firm Morning Consult.

They are pursuing millennial dollars. Actively.

Disney offers adults-only cruises. Even in its mixed family-cruise lines, the company offers separate areas for adults-only pools, lounges and nightclubs to offer parents respite from their active children.

What would Walt Do? What does this have to do with your business?

Repeat after me... EVERYTHING

First, this is a powerful reminder of the brand loyalty guests have to Disney. Disney's return / repeat rate is over 75%. Four generations of families are now entering the parks.

Now would be a good time to calculate your repeat rate.

How is it?

What are you doing to increase it?

Second, Disney shows us how they market to every sub-niche they have in their global market. Millennials have gobs of cash (due to better paying jobs and saving money by sleeping in their parents basements).

⇒ Do you have a separate and distinct marketing system for your niches and sub-niches?

Disney does it with their cruises. In my carpet business, we have separate marketing systems for cat owners, dog owners, homes with children, older adults, etc...

⇒ Can you create separate products / services for your sub-niches? And of course, price it accordingly?

Finally, Disney has publicity that it has not paid for.

They didn't even start this whole kerfuffle. Someone just made a post, and BAM! off it went.

⇒ Are your clients or patients so in tune with you, so enamored with your service, so loyal to your product, that they would come to your rescue if there was a negative story about you?

⇒ Are you creating passion for your business? I have fanatics who preach my carpet cleaning gospel. This was cultivated through years of personal and consistent touches with my clients.

Take the time now, to really dig into how your clients feel about your company.

Do you have raving fans or raving lunatics?

Low prices:
An indicator of poor service?

W ell... I have a confession to make. And it is pretty embarrassing. I did not follow my own advice.

The temptation of a low price, and then the acceptance of that low price as a buyer is like being addicted to crack (or so I am told). You say to yourself, *"I'll just do it once"*.

Low price shopping is an addiction

Let me relate a little story to you that happened to me just this week, and boy did I get burned by not following my own advice.

As many of you know, in addition to being a Disney Way and Marketing Strategist, I also own an Oriental Rug and Carpet Cleaning business on the Eastern Shore of Maryland.

I have a few vans on the road that each travel about 30-35,000 miles every year. As you can imagine, that is a lot of oil changes and new tires.

I used to buy the tires for my vans at the best tire center in the area. But with the mileage we put on them, I was spending almost TWO GRAND a year in tires.

I thought, there has to be another way.

Moving to the "dark side"

Well a new tire company came into town and offered "used" tires at a ridiculously low price. Against my better judgement, I took their bait and started down the dark path of buying on the criteria of price alone.

I started buying "gently used" tires for the vans. I was lured in by the low price (about 40 bucks a tire) which beat buying four new tires at about $180.00 each.

But there always seemed to be a problem. The alignment would be out of whack, the vans would have a weird rumble, or there was an odd bubble on the tire. The tire company would always replace the tire, no charge, but it became a hassle.

Stuck on the "dark side"

Then I started to notice other things that were happening in their store, mainly being left on hold for an eternity with no promise (or hope) of anyone returning to pick up the phone.

The front desk person was surly at best, more like snarly and rude.

The shop was usually in disarray with tools, oils, fluids, and kitty litter all over the shop floor. I should have bailed out right then and there...

But I was hooked on price, like a junky on crack.

But we all have our breaking point.

Last week I got a panicked call from one of my employees, *"Boss, the rear tire just blew out and there are hunks of it all over the highway". Are you ok? "Yep"* he said.

Well change the tire, I told him. *"The spare is stuck, I can't get it down".* OK, ok... So I gave the cheapo company a call to try to get some help.

Surly lady answers the phone *"Hello"*. No mention of the company name, her name or even a pleasant greeting.

"Is this P&R tires?" I asked. *"Yep"* she states.

"One of my vans is stuck about 10 miles from your shop, can you send a truck out?"

"Let me check" was the last thing I heard for the next 3 minutes.

I hung up and called back 2 more times and was placed on hold for a total of at least 7 minutes. Finally on the 4th call, surly lady said *"Can't you hold?!"*

By this time I was driving out to the stranded van to help my employee get the spare tire that was stuck under the van. On my way, I called the BEST tire company in town, the one I had been lured away from by the cheapo price.

"One of my vans is broken down on the highway and he can't get the spare disconnected from the hold".

The first words out of her mouth were *"Brent can be there in 15 minutes and help you out".*

My jaw dropped.

How could I have been so stupid as to be lured away from these guys?

To make me feel even more guilty, she continued *"We help ALL of our best customers, don't you worry".*

Me? A Schmuck?

Well I felt like a total schmuck.

I could not bring myself to confess my sin of leaving them for a cheaper competitor. After Brent got down there, he managed to dislodge the spare tire and get us on our way.

We shook hands and he said *"Great to see you again Mr. Morris, glad we could help you out today".*

Sheepishly I thanked him and told him I would be in the next day to have the tire repaired.

By the end of the week, I had spent, no... invested, in new tires for all of my vehicles. About two grand in all.

I never felt better...

So... is low price always an indicator of poor service? Maybe not always, but it is damn sure a powerful indicator:

⇒ Walmart vs. Nordstroms

⇒ McDonalds vs Ruth's Chris Steak House

⇒ Hershey Park vs Disney

⇒ Motel 6 vs. Four Seasons

I will let the comparisons speak for themselves.

I bet my Daughters Girl Scout Troop has better phone scripts than you do!

When my 7 year old daughter, Emma, joined our local girl scout troop. My wife and I thought it would a good character building organization to belong to and would help reinforce what we were teaching her at home.

Now as most of you know, I coach other businesses how to implement Disney style service and monetize it through direct response marketing.

My kids hear me speak about it all of the time. I have all manner of CD's playing in the car; Dan Kennedy, Chet Holmes, Brian Tracy... just to name a few.

To say they are getting another education traveling in Dad's car would be an understatement.

Professional Sales Organization

But little did I know that my daughter would be joining a "professional sales organization"!

I have had all of my kids in some sort of activity or sport where they were required to fund raise to help defray the costs.

But none of them come close to the Girl Scouts fund raising sales machine.

Not the Cub Scouts.

Not the local soccer club.

Nor the chess club or ballet studio.

After the first meeting Emma came home with something to sell her family, friends and relatives.

Did you catch that?

"The very first meeting"!!!

They are setting the stage right from the beginning that raising money is a prime objective of the girl scouts. But here is what separated the girl scouts from the rest of the nonprofit bunch my kids belong to...

She brought home SCRIPTS!

The title of the sales program (selling magazine subscription vouchers) was the "59 minute Quick Start". Even the Girl Scouts have a "Quick Start" program to get them working together and indoctrinated into the group.

This program was designed to be completed during the regular troop meeting in less than an hour.

They also have a GOAL SHEET that they had to fill out before they started dialing for dollars. It listed out friends, family, distant family, neighbors, parents co-workers (damn... no affiliate commissions here) and friends at church.

Yep... They have real, live scripts that had everything written out for them to sell a ton of magazines. The opening paragraph was a standard introduction stating their name, what they were selling and the sales goal they had set.

After her spiel, the final line was not "would you like to buy" which is a question just begging for a "No" answer.

Nope, the question at the end was an assumptive close

"How many vouchers would you like to buy?"

There is a big lesson here.

Too many phone operators are still using yes or no questions that are just a "no" waiting to happen.

⇒ Take a clue from the scouts and examine your scripts for these no-waiting-to-happen questions.

If the prospect says "Yes", they are not merely order takers, nooooo... they go right into an UPSELL script by telling the prospect they can be a MVP if they get the 3 pack for just $45.

My daughter added her own flair to it by saying *"You do want to be a MVP, don't you?"* Nothing like being made feel small and un-manly by a seven year old. *"Of course I was going to be an MVP"!*

If the prospect says no, the scout has a DOWNSELL script for that.

They ask *"would you like to buy one voucher and donate it to charity"*?

If the prospect still said no, they would thank for their time and move on. There was lots of dialing-for-dollars happening at this meeting.

Of course, I do need to report on the results.

- My daughter made 17 phone calls using the scripts provided.
- She closed 13 of the 17!!!
- To make it even more exciting, she got 9 of the 17 to take the upsell!

I see a tremendous sales career in her future. She was the #2 salesperson, I mean girl scout, in her troop.

She made this salesman Daddy very proud.

So... I know you are just waiting to ask...

What does this have to do with your business?

Altogether now and in unison... EVERYTHING!

Take the time right now to go inspect your phone and live scripts:

⇒ Do you have daily, weekly, hourly sales quota's?

⇒ Do your phone people have goals to achieve?

⇒ Do they have the right scripts?

⇒ Are they following and adhering to the scripts?

If my daughter can do it; following the super simple scripts provided by the girl scouts **and** have a closing rate north of 75% **and** an UPSELL rate of more than 50%, than you can have the same success as well.

Go NOW and inspect your scripts and your employee's adherence to them. It could be the difference between losing money or phenomenal profits in your business.

Me? Not Nice? I Just Want The Toilet to Work!

L ast Thanksgiving, my family and I decided to boycott turkey and our relatives and head off on a 2 day vacation at a nearby resort.

For the price and location, I would have expected more from the resort. I even created a Facebook post while I waited 30 minutes in line just to check in.

Yep! 30 minutes just to check in!

They only had 4 employees checking in guests. There were 8 open stations with no one working.

The wait was so long, I had my wife go get me a beer while I waited in line.

You would think that a company as large as the Gaylord would know that the day before a holiday would be busy.

We even over heard an employee say "*we didn't think it would be this busy*".

Evidently, my post touched a nerve in a few of my FB followers, suggesting that I be "nice" to the workers.

Of course I was going to be nice! But if I ran into a manager, I am afraid my snarkiness would come out.

By the way we never did see a member of management the whole time we were there.

At some point during our stay, one of my kids clogged the toilet in the room and water went everywhere. I went an found a house keeper who said they would call engineering immediately.

Evidently, a clogged toilet in a guest room with water flowing on the floor is not a top priority.

Three hours later we still had water all over the floor.

I then called the front desk who said they would be "right there".

Nuthin!

It would be easy to blame the employees. It would be easy to blame the line level managers. But, I am afraid, the problem runs deeper.

I suspect there is no direction or vision from the top of the organization explaining the expectations of the resort.

What does this have to do with your business?

EVERYTHING!

Let's start at the top!

The 30 minute wait to check in... Maybe they had a lot of employees call out sick. It happens. But what was their contingency plan?

Evidently, they did not have one.

What could they have done?

⇒ A manager could have been walking the line talking to guests.

⇒ A manager could have alerted the Food & Beverage department who could have sent a server over with a tray of champagne, brownies or something.

⇒ A manager could have asked the entertainment department to have the little musical trio move to the front desk area.

⇒ Management could have handed out a coupon for a free drink or dessert. Better yet, management could have empowered the employees to do so.

How about that clogged toilet?

⇒ Again, it was a holiday weekend and they knew it would be busy. Having extra engineers on staff would have helped.

⇒ Trusting the housekeepers with a toilet plunger would have immediately solved that issue.

Are my expectations too high?
I think not.

It is criminal that they management of this resort was in hiding.

Do you or your team "hide" when there is an issue?

Do you have a contingency plan for when things go wrong?

When I was at Disney, the management team was in the trenches with the line level cast members, especially when things were not going well. We took responsibility and we turned what could be a bad experience into a good one.

Never be boring, never be stale. Plus it like Disney

A re you boring?

Worse, has your business become stale, and boring?

Do your clients feel a wow effect when they enter your business or have you enter their home?

Clients can become bored with your business faster than Buzz Lightyear leaping to infinity and beyond.

And that is not good.

A bored client will go elsewhere. It will not have anything to do with your service or product, they are just bored.

This is one of the TOP 3 reasons a client or customer will leave you, according to Dan Kennedy, a world renowned copywriter and marketer.

Why do you think that companies keep introducing new and improved soap, detergent, toothpaste, chicken sandwiches or teeth cleaning?

To keep their customers and clients interested in their product or service and to keep them coming back for more.

New and improved is one of the main driving forces at the Walt Disney company.

We are constantly reviewing our performance and metrics and making adjustments to improve.

Recently, I had custom "fringe combs" made for my rug business. A fringe comb is just a hair pick designed to comb the fringe on your rug. Mine were customized with a logo and phone number. Now every client who has fringe will get a comb.

Walt Disney called this "*plussing*". You see, he envisioned the parks as evolving and ever changing to meet the demands of today's guests.

You must do the same with your business.

In an interview with Walt Disney back in 1956, he first brought up the concept of plussing the show. *"It is something that will never be finished... I want something that is alive, something that could grow, something I could keep plussing with ideas... I can change the parks because it is alive"*.

In fact, Walt did not wait long to begin plussing his shows and attractions.

In 1957, a mere two years after the Jungle Cruise in Disneyland opened, he plussed the

show by adding a campsite overrun by gorillas and the trader Sam shrunken head.

He continued to plus by introducing the water spraying elephants in 1962 and the addition of the snapping crocodiles in 1976.

In an article by Brady McDonald, Walt Disney imagineer (the creative guys and gals that dream up the rides, attractions and resorts) Scott Towbridge, was quoted:

"the key to plussing is to strike a balance between new and old. It is not about adding new technology just for the whiz bang effect, but asking if there are new ways of telling the story".

Plussing the show has been an enduring and perpetual way of life throughout the Disney company for its 60 plus year existence

In my own businesses we continue to add and tweak how we deliver our services.

For the summer, the crews wear Hawaiian shirts, and say aloha. It is virtually certain, that no other carpet cleaning company within 1,000 miles of me is doing this.

And the clients love it.

We also change up our post cleaning gifts. For May and June, we give out grill tool sets as part of our summer promotions.

Plusing your clients experience does not need to be drastic or overly expensive.

Small incremental, but noticeable changes will suffice.

⇒ Is it a uniform change?

⇒ New promotion?

⇒ A paint job?

⇒ New signage?

⇒ New videos in the lobby?

⇒ Current magazines in the waiting room?

Take a walk around with a few of your team.

⇒ Look for areas that could be improved, changed or plussed.

⇒ Then you need to take action. Yes... You need to do something.

⇒ Once you have made the change, be sure that you make a big deal out of it and announce it to your clients and prospects.

⇒ Throw a party or open house. Invite in a local politician (they love this kind of stuff).

Why I paid more for my hammer

Have you ever passed by one store that was close to you or more convenient and go out of your way to purchase the same item at a store further away and less convenient?

I find myself doing it all the time now as my tolerance for poor service is in its death throws. I guess this is just one of the ways that I am combating the insidious decline in customer service... TAKING MY MONEY ELSWHERE.

During my last effort at home improvement I needed a new hammer as I had misplaced the old one.

So off the LOCAL hardware store I went, which is about 15 miles from the house and right past one of those big box home improvement center (not Home Depot, the other one).

Yep that other center is only about 3 miles from the house and I happily zoomed past it. Why?

Yes they were closer, but that did not matter.

Yes they had better, more convenient parking, but that did not sway me from my mission.

You see, their service absolutely SUCKS.

They have a greeter at the front door who does NOT do his job title, not once have they greeted me or the people I walked in the store with.

Most of the employees are clueless (read that as UNTRAINED) and could not find the hammer if it was in their sightline.

This is the same store where I had my first of many wordless transactions. *Check out my book "Systematic Magic" for the full story.*

The cashiers, with great frequency, would not speak unless spoken to.

During my unscientific test, the cashier would not say one word to me unless I said something first 5 out of 9 times. No "good morning", no "did you find everything?", nuthin, zip, nada.

Don't get me wrong, they TRY to provide a few little extras, like cold stale coffee for contractors. But the execution of these little extras falls woefully flat.

But I drive right past this place and try to find parking on the street by the local hardware store.

Now compare this to my LOCALLY owned hardware store

Instead of the free parking, I have to feed a meter with a quarter and walk two blocks. Not convenient, but a small price to pay for the service and treatment I will soon experience.

When you walk it the first thing that gets your attention is the aroma of fresh brewed coffee.

Two cashiers who say *"good morning"* almost in unison and offer me a cup of fresh coffee.

They are hanging out with a few other customers at the counter. If there weren't tools everywhere, you would think they were hanging in Starbucks.

One of them then ask if I caught the game last night. "*Yep*" I answer, "our Easton Warriors crushed the Queen Anne Lions" (we are talking local football, not NFL).

While they don't know my name (hey this is not Cheers), they do recognize me as a past customer. "*What can we help you with today?*", one asks.

I explain my project and let them know I need a hammer and some special nails.

"*Right this way*" and begins to walk me over to the tool aisle. He did not point to an aisle or just give me directions, he walked me to the hammers.

I of course notice the prices, and I know that they are about 20% higher than the big box store. But I do not say a word.

I am getting exactly what I am paying for.

He walks me back to the register and asks if I need anything else and I say I don't.

After the transaction is complete and the register drawer is closed, he asks where I parked.

After I tell him he pulls out an old coffee can with the words "PARKING QUARTERS" written on the side. He pulls out TWO quarters and says *"One for today and one for the next time"*. WOW! I was blown away!

I leave happier than when I arrived.

So... what's my hammer have to do with your business?

Everything!!!

My local hardware store is the Disney of hammer sellers. They get it right on so many levels.

You would think they were my clients or read my book *Systematic Magic*. But they have been long at this level of service since well before I was born.

First, they have the WOW factor down.

Fresh coffee and an aggressively friendly greeting (Disney speak for how their cast members should behave) from two of the employees.

Not the owners, but the employees.

Here are two HUGE points for you to implement in your business.

⇒ What can you do to WOW your clients?

⇒ It can be as simple as offering a cup of coffee. And are you training your employees to be "aggressively friendly"? Not over bearing, but genuine, caring and helpful?

True to Disney form, the employee WALKED me TO the hammers, not merely pointing down a long aisle.

⇒ Do your employees merely point, gesture or grunt to your hard earned clients?

Truer to Disney form

are the prices.

Everyone know that a rubber ball at Disney is going to be at least 10x more expensive than the same ball at Wal-Mart.

Sure their hammer was about 20% more, but I was already immersed in an experience where price was almost irrelevant.

Now TRUEST to Disney form was the quarter jar that they implemented for parking.

They had not done this in the past, but they recognized that this was an area where their competitor had an edge.

They "PLUSSED" their experience with the SIMPLE and COST EFFECTIVE solution of handing out quarters.

They did not need a mangers approval, they had the authority to take care of their customers.

This will certainly NOT break their bank and will probably earn them many customers for life.

⇒ What small, incremental improvements can you make in your business to PLUS your show?

Warning:

The next chapter has a joke that some may find offensive.

Turn the page at your own risk.

Author is not responsible for your reaction or the hilarity of said joke.

Sex after surgery...

A recent article in the Kentucky Post reported that a woman, one Anne Maynard, has sued St Luke's hospital, saying that after her husband had surgery there, he lost all interest in sex.

A hospital spokesman replied ... "*Mr. Maynard was admitted in Ophthalmology – all we did was correct his eyesight.*"

Ok... So that was NOT one of the funniest jokes to ever be told. But there is a point or two I would like to make.

⇒ Is your "eyesight" blurry and out of focus?

⇒ What are you seeing or not seeing in your business?

⇒ And are you blaming others for your poor vision?

BillyBob The Ignoramus

I had a call yesterday with a fellow business owner who seems to only call when his business is slow and he can't explain it.

BillyBob (real name not used to protect the ignoramus) says, "*I think it is the weather that is affecting my sales, but it might be the month*".

Now, having had this SAME conversation with BillyBob a hundred times over the past few years I knew that he had not implemented any of the strategies I had given him for FREE!

Maybe if I charged him, he might have implemented.

So knowing full well what the answers would be I asked:

⇒ Do you have a structured method for gathering and responding to prospects?

⇒ Do you have your Service Vision and Standards Developed?

⇒ Are you creating a titanium cage around your current clients so that they don't leave and you keep the competition out?

After 4 years of off and on again (mostly off) conversations, he had yet to implement a single strategy and wanted to know WHY things sucked as bad as they did.

He continued to complain about slow sales, poor employees, price shoppers and cheap-skates. I had to get off the phone with him.

It is later than you think

Have you been given a proven money making strategy and then done nothing with it?

Why?

What are you waiting for?

Go find that strategy right now.

Stop reading and go get it.

Yes, You!

Right Now!

Ok... welcome back. Now that you have that strategy in your hands, IMPLEMENT IT!

Don't wait another second.

Do it NOW!

Worst Guarantee EVER!

Recently, I took my kids to the local McDonald's for milkshakes (which is about the only thing I will let them eat there). As we were waiting in line at the drive through window, I noticed a sign posted crooked, which read:

"Accuracy Guarantee. We get it right, or we make it right. If you place an order and don't get the correct items, we'll make it right."

www.DeliverServiceNow.com

The worst guarantee EVER

My first reaction was *"**That is the dumbest freakin' thing I have ever seen.**"*

Come on... I would certainly hope and expect my order to be correct and for McDonald's to fix it, if it was not correct.

My next reaction was, I wonder what "make it right" means to the employees at this particular restaurant?

Would I get something Free?

Would they offer me a gift card for a return visit?

Maybe offer me a free coffee for my trouble?

So I decided to ask when I got to the cashier. I placed my order for 4 chocolate shakes.

The cashier said she had NEVER seen the sign and had no idea what it meant!

Score one for poor management communication.

So I paid the lady at the first window and moved on the second window to pick up my order.

Of course, I was now amused at the situation, so I asked the second McDonald's employee *"What does the Accuracy Guarantee mean?"*

Of course, he had no clue.

He had never seen the sign.

Score one more for poor management

As we drove away, my son called from the back seat *"<u>Dad, my cup has a hole in it and it is leaking all over me and the car</u>."*

Sure enough, my son was covered in GREEN goo. Not only did his cup have a leak in it, but they had given him one of those green minty shakes....

So we parked in the lot and went in the restaurant to get cleaned up. While my son was in the bathroom, I went to find the manager to complain about the cup and the incorrect flavors.

He was more than happy to exchange the shakes, but offered no apology about the leaky cup, my kids sticky clothes or the mess in the back seat of my car. So I decided to test the guarantee.

I asked him "*What about your make-it-right guarantee?*" He just looked at me like I had three heads and had just spoken a foreign language.

"*What are you talking about?*" he asked. I then escorted him to the window and showed him his sign.

"*I have never seen that before*" he exclaimed. "*My district manager must have put that there and not told us.*"

SCORE!!! A perfect trifecta of poor communication by the management of this store.

And with that he turned and walked into the kitchen, never to reappear.

What's this got to do with your business? All together now... EVERYTHING!

⇒ First, please examine your guarantee. Have someone else outside of your family and business read it and have them tell you what it means to them. You may be surprised by the answer.

⇒ Secondly, if you don't have a guarantee, it is high time that you created one. It will set you apart from your competition. Make sure it is bold and meaningful.

⇒ Then test it on a few people and get their reaction. Make any tweeks as you see necessary.

⇒ Finally, be sure to communicate your guarantee to your entire team as well as publicizing for the public. Make sure your staff understands the guarantee and how they should react when it is tested.

When I was at the Disney Company, we held multiple staff meetings throughout the day to ensure that all cast members were up to date on our policies.

You have your home work assignment, go do it NOW!

About Vance "The Crypt Keeper" Morris

Vance spent 10 years working for the mouse at Walt Disney World in Orlando Florida. He started his career at Disney on the Opening Team of the Yacht & Beach Club Resorts, and progressed through the management ranks as a Night Club Manager at Pleasure Island, Service Trainer aboard the Empress Lily, and on the revitalization team of the Contemporary Resort in the mid-90's.

It was at the Contemporary that Vance got his crowning achievement, Designing, Opening and Operating Chef Mickey's, Disney's flagship Character Dining Experience.

After leaving Disney, (yes people do leave) he utilized his skills to rescue or improve many of America's companies and government agencies.

His clients included Legal Seafoods, Tyson, NASA, Rain Forest Café, Compass Group, The Executive Office of the President of the United States, The Smithsonian and the Kennedy Center for the Performing Arts.

Tiring of corporate life, Vance opened his own Bricks & Mortar Business in 2007. After meteoric growth of his service business, other entrepreneurs began to seek him out for advice and counsel. This spawned his next business, Deliver Service Now!, consulting and coaching other companies on how to create and implement Disney style service and then apply Direct Response Marketing to profit from it.

Vance Morris has shared the stage with many of the premier marketers and service professional in the world; Dan Kennedy, Joe Polish, Bob Brown, Lou Ferrigno, Dean Jackson, Charles Henning, Lee Cockerell, and Meg Crofton.

Vance Fulfilled Dreams & Generated Profits at Disney

He can do the same for you

Vance has limited openings throughout the year where he will work 1:1 with select businesses creating a Customized Systematic MAGIC Service & Marketing Plan.

Or do you need a dynamic, entertaining and expert speaker for a presentation or conference? Visit: www.VanceMorris.com

Send Vance a fax request to 410-697-6072 with the following information:

- Decision makers name

- Business name

- Snail mail address

- Email address

- Phone number

- Project as you envision it (Client Service Strategies, Speaking, Marketing review/ analysis, etc)

- Required completion date, if any

A response can be expected within 72 hours.

P.S. Want to mortify your 8 year old daughter? Get your picture taken with all of the Disney princesses.

Cinderella & I

Rapunzel & I

Snow White & I

Ariel & I

Resources:

The Book: *Systematic Magic. 7 Magic Keys to Disnify Your Business. How to Out Serve, Out Price and Out Market Your Competition in Ant Economy*

Available at Amazon.com

The Course: My 3-day Disney Boot Camp to build your Disney-style business. DVD's, CD's, Workbooks, Templates and Blueprints.

Available at:
www.DeliverServiceNow.com

FREE MONEY MAKING GIFTS

FREE Systematic Magic Report

FREE Live Webcasts— with the Crypt Keeper

FREE E-mail Newsletter—A valuable and entertaining strategy or tactic in every issue.

All resources mentioned in the book can be found at:

www.DeliverServiceNow.com

NOTES:

_____

_____

_____

_____

_____

_____

_____

_____

_____

_____

_____

_____

_____

Made in the USA
Monee, IL
02 July 2020